Saving the Amazon
TOGETHER

Rob Waring, *Series Editor*

HEINLE
CENGAGE Learning

Australia • Brazil • Japan • Korea • Mexico • Singapore • Spain • United Kingdom • United States

Words to Know

This story is set in the South American country of Brazil. It takes place in the Amazon rain forest.

 Amazon Rain Forest at Risk. Read the paragraph. Then match each word with the correct definition.

The rain forests of the Amazon region are experiencing a crisis. They are quickly being destroyed by extensive deforestation resulting from human development. The rain forest is also being used for illegal hydraulic mining operations to find precious metals like gold. The method erodes the soil and fills the rivers with silt. The mercury used in the process also poisons wildlife and creates health risks. Now, a team of experts is helping the wardens of the newly formed Tumucumaque [tumukumɑki] National Park fight off illegal foresting and mining operations.

1. crisis _____	**a.** operated by the pressure of water
2. deforestation _____	**b.** a disaster; an emergency
3. hydraulic _____	**c.** the action of clearing an area of trees
4. erode _____	**d.** loose sand, mud, and soil
5. silt _____	**e.** wear away; wash away
6. mercury _____	**f.** a person who cares for something
7. warden _____	**g.** a metallic element that has a liquid, shiny appearance

deforestation

2

B The Disappearing Rain Forest.
Read these facts about the Amazon rain forest. Then write the basic form of the underlined word or phrase next to each definition.

- Some people consider the beautiful forests of the Amazon region to be paradise.
- Experts estimate that 137 plant, animal, and insect species—many of which are rare and exotic—become extinct every single day.
- In Brazil alone, more than 90 local tribes have disappeared since the 1900s.
- At least 3,000 indigenous fruits grow in the rain forests; of these only 200 are used in the rest of the world, while native peoples of the rain forest use over 2,000.

1. a perfect place, often considered to be imaginary: _____

2. native to a region: _____

3. unusual in a positive manner: _____

4. a group of people who usually speak the same language, live in the same area, often in villages, and have many relatives within the group: _____

warden

erode

silt

mercury

An Illegal Hydraulic Mining Operation

3

Brazil is one of the largest countries in the world. It offers an enormous Atlantic coastline as well as some of the world's greatest rivers. Its most famous river—the huge and powerful Amazon—is one of the world's longest, carrying an estimated 20 percent, or one fifth, of the world's fresh water.

Brazil is also home to the Amazon **tropical**[1] rain forest. The Amazon rain forest is populated by millions of different types of insects, plants, animals, and birds, many of which are exotic and rare. The diversity of plant species found here is the highest on Earth, with some experts estimating that one square kilometer* may contain over 75,000 types of trees and 150,000 species of plants. It has the largest collection of plant and animal species in the world. One in five of all the birds on Earth lives in the rain forests of the Amazon. In fact, there are so many different species living in the Amazon rain forest, that scientists have yet to record all of them. However, despite the rare species and the beautiful landscape, the Amazon is far from being a paradise, and there are a number of threats to its future survival.

---

[1]**tropical:** geographically located between the Tropic of Cancer and the Tropic of Capricorn
*See page 48 for metric conversion chart.

 CD 3, Track 05

The threats surrounding the Amazon region are considerable enough to classify the situation as a crisis. Its rain forests are quickly being destroyed by the widespread deforestation resulting from human settlement and land development. The **wholesale**[2] clearing and exploitation of land for settlement and industry, including mining, has made the situation critical.

Help to save the Amazon rain forest is needed now more than ever. While the deforestation of the Amazon region is significant on a local and ecological basis, it is also important on a global basis. Due to its importance within the world's ecological systems, the Amazon region is of vital importance to the future of our planet and to the future of the human race. Therefore, a concerned group of people have been brought together to travel deep into the rain forest in an effort to help save it.

---

[2]**wholesale:** extensive; massive

Skim for Gist

Read through the entire book quickly to answer the questions.

1. What is the reader basically about?

2. What does the group mentioned on page 8 do to help the rain forest?

Help to prevent the seemingly inevitable destruction of the Amazon rain forest arrives via the great river itself. It comes in the form of an expedition team of scientists and other conservation experts. As the team travels by boat up the Amazon River, it becomes obvious that it's a varied group of people, all from different places and different organizations. However they are united by a single ultimate goal: saving the rain forests of the Amazon.

The expedition team has come deep into the rain forest with a purpose: to clearly define the borders and the rules of a newly created national park, known as Tumucumaque. The park is enormous—about 3.8 million hectares in size—but it only employs five people. There are not nearly enough staff members to properly take care of the more remote sections of the huge park. Quite simply, the park needs people to help safely and securely establish the park's operational systems.

Tumucumaque is approximately 3.8 million hectares, or almost 15,000 square miles, in size.

The Brazilian government established the new national park as a legal entity and allocated funds for its administration. However, giving a new park legal existence through legislation is one thing, creating a park on the ground and making it a reality is quite another. The first step for the expedition is to begin the long task of marking the borders of the park. They must stop at strategic points along the huge waterway to put up large signs announcing that the surrounding area has been registered as a national park. At one point, one of the team members even hangs from a tree in order to hang a sign at a height from which it will be easily visible from the river.

Besides marking the borders of the huge section of land, another major issue that the park legislators will need to deal with is monitoring the park. The area is simply so vast that it is going to be extremely difficult to regulate effectively. Its borders will have to be **patrolled**[3] regularly to ensure that miners and other people don't illegally cross over the border into the protected park area and cause destruction. That's why this team of experts has made the journey to help develop a plan for structuring the park's ongoing administration effectively.

---

[3]**patrol:** make regular trips around an area or along a border line to guard against trouble or crime

The World Wildlife Fund (WWF)
works to raise the world's
awareness of environmental issues.

The team is part of the Amazon Region Protected Areas (ARPA) program, one of the largest and most ambitious conservation projects in history. This program, created and run by a panel of conservation experts, intends to one day create parks and reserves totaling an area the size of the U.S. state of California—about 42 million hectares—across the vital Amazon region. The APRA is well aware of the fact that creating parks and other protected areas is probably the only way to realistically save the Amazon region.

The experts gathered for the team that will help set up Tumucumaque come from the different organizations involved with the project. Claudio Maretti has come from the World Wildlife Fund (WWF), a large environmental organization that works to protect wildlife around the world. Maretti is joined by **Christoph Jaster**,[4] a Brazilian government park warden, and **Jawapuku Wayapi**,[5] a member of one of the indigenous people living on lands neighboring the park. When asked why the group was formed, Maretti simply replies, "Somebody needs to come here and do the job, and that's what we're doing."

---

[4] **Christoph Jaster:** [krɪstɔf yastər]
[5] **Jawapuku Wayapi:** [dʒɑwɑpu̱ku wɑyɑ̱pi]

The expedition's mission here is twofold. First, they are searching for criminals, such as illegal gold miners who may be harming this precious, newly protected landscape. Second, they are serving on somewhat of a **diplomatic**[6] mission, seeking understanding and cooperation with the neighboring tribes that live alongside the park's lands. They hope to convince these native peoples to work with them side by side to establish and protect the park's borders.

As the expedition travels deep into the rain forest, the group stops from time to time to speak with people from the indigenous tribes. As they do so, they spend time explaining the program, listening to questions, and above all, suggesting ways in which they could all work together with a common purpose. Jawapuku Wayapi says that by working with each other, the authorities and his people can protect the new park from being invaded by illegal commercial activity.

At one point, the team takes a moment to examine a large map. From here on out, the journey will become even more challenging as they move into the more remote and untraveled areas of the forest. They inspect the complicated drawing for a long period of time, trying to chart the best route through the region. Finally, the decision about where to go is made. The expedition is then joined by some indigenous tribe members as they continue their exploration along the wild and exotic river.

---

[6]**diplomatic:** showing skill at handling people sensitively

The ARPA program hopes to work with the indigenous peoples of the Amazon region to save the rain forests.

There are no roads in this remote area of the park, and few **airstrips**,[7] so it wasn't an option for Maretti and his team to fly in. Water is the most efficient and practical way to travel through this part of the Amazon region, but it's not an easy journey for the team. They must go against the **current**[8] the majority of the time, and in some cases this is quite dangerous. One false move or error in judgment and the small boats in which they're riding could easily be upset and any one of their members could find himself in the waters of the huge river. At certain points along the way, the team must stop, get out, and attach ropes to the sides of their boats so that they can pull them over rocky or fast-flowing areas.

---

[7] **airstrip:** a long thin stretch of road for landing aircraft
[8] **current:** the flow of water in the river

Water is often the most efficient and practical way to travel.

In the past, the dangerous currents and majestic waterfalls in this region have stopped all but a few explorers and fortune seekers from coming here. As the team **paddles**[9] further up the river, they eventually arrive at a barrier that would stop most explorers: an enormous waterfall. The team takes time to examine the situation. Any way they look at it, there's not going to be an easy way to get around it. At this point, even the team leader Claudio Maretti is frustrated. "This is the largest **obstacle**,[10] [and] the most important we have to cross," he reports. If the team wants to continue their journey up the Amazon, it means that they're going to have to somehow get the boats uphill to the top of the waterfall.

---

[9]**paddle:** move a boat with a paddle, a tool with a handle ending in a broad, flat, or slightly curved surface
[10]**obstacle:** something that gets in the way and stops action or progress

Scan for Information

Scan page 21 to find the information.

1. How does the team manage to get the boats to the top of the waterfall?

2. How many of them are involved in the task?

3. How long does it take to complete the task?

After some time and consideration, the team finally realizes that there are only two things that can help them continue their journey: strength and brains. They decide to construct a **pulley**[11] system using ropes and wheels in order to get the boats to the top of the waterfall. The ropes are attached to the boats and then the entire team has to work together to pull each boat up the hillside using the pulley system. Each person holds on to a rope and pulls hard. As they do, the ropes turn within the system and slowly move the huge, heavy wooden boats up the side of the hill. It's extremely hard work and takes several hours, but eventually the team is successful. With a lot of effort, they've managed to get the boats to the top of the waterfall, but it's not yet the end of their difficult journey. Some of the biggest challenges for the group are still to come.

---

[11] **pulley:** a device used to lift or lower heavy objects

After their heavy lifting, the team is exhausted, but they still need to continue moving forward, and what they have ahead of them may make the waterfall look easy. Park warden Christoph Jaster wants to find a gold mine he has seen from the air. According to his **GPS**,[12] the mine should be nearby, and they should be able to see a way into it from the river. Jaster has made it a priority for the team to find the gold mine and see what they can do about stopping the illegal operation.

In order to accomplish the task of locating the mine in a huge, thick forest of trees, the team must rely on their GPS and experience. As they move slowly along the banks of the river, Claudio Maretti explains their relatively simple plan, "We're going back to try to find an entrance–a small river or a track in the forest." Once they've found the track that the miners have been using to traffic their goods and supplies, the team will simply need to follow it to its source: the illegal mine.

---

[12] **GPS:** Global Positioning System; an electronic system that assists in locating places and objects

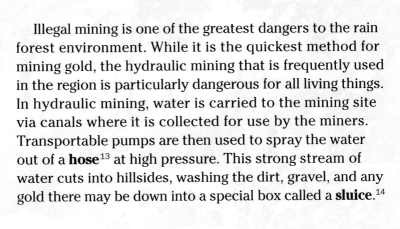

Illegal mining is one of the greatest dangers to the rain forest environment. While it is the quickest method for mining gold, the hydraulic mining that is frequently used in the region is particularly dangerous for all living things. In hydraulic mining, water is carried to the mining site via canals where it is collected for use by the miners. Transportable pumps are then used to spray the water out of a **hose**[13] at high pressure. This strong stream of water cuts into hillsides, washing the dirt, gravel, and any gold there may be down into a special box called a **sluice**.[14]

Due to the scale of production and speed of extraction, this method of mining has severe and long-lasting environmental impacts. It erodes the soil, which causes loss of rain forest area. It also creates silt in rivers, which can negatively affect the habitats of the countless different species of plants and animals living in the river. However, the most dangerous aspect of the process is the mercury used to extract the gold. Mercury is an extremely unsafe substance that can poison wildlife and create health risks for neighboring indigenous communities. In addition, it can take years to be washed out of an ecological system, and its long-lasting effects can be damaging for a very long time.

---

[13] **hose:** a long tube that carries liquids
[14] **sluice:** an artificial water channel with an open end for controlling water flow

Preventing gold mining in the delicate and valuable environment of the Amazon rain forest is a high priority on almost everyone's agenda. The ARPA program is trying to establish innovative partnerships with the indigenous peoples of the area to meet their objectives. In the case of the Tumucumaque National Park, authorities hope to create a partnership with the local Wayapi tribe. The organization intends to supply the indigenous group with both boats and fuel so that they can help patrol the new park's borders. According to Claudio Maretti, this is an unusual **collaboration**,[15] but obviously one that could benefit both sides involved. It encourages the tribe members to take part in protecting their own environment as well as to work toward making illegal gold mining more difficult.

---

[15] **collaboration:** a varied group working towards the same goal

While plans are in the works for implementing programs to stop illegal mining in the rain forests of the park, for the moment the gold mining continues. Consequently, the expedition team is trying to uncover signs of prohibited mines as they travel up the Amazon. Far up the river, the team thinks they may have found what they have been looking for: a path that appears to have been made by miners. Together with an armed police unit, they follow the path deep into the forest. As they pass through the thick trees, they begin to find evidence of mining: abandoned machinery parts and other signs of human influence. Eventually, as they get closer to the suspected mining site, the team comes across a frightened miner named Francisco. After some convincing, the man agrees to lead them several miles into the forest to the gold mine for which they've been searching.

Once at the mining site, the team realizes the degree of damage from just one mining operation. As they survey the cleared space in the forest, they can see the remains of what was once probably a relatively large operation, but one that has become slowly smaller over the years. The equipment and machinery used to extract the gold lies all around the site. Throughout the entire clearing, there are signs of significant damage to the environment including land entirely cleared of trees and large dirty pools of water.

After inspecting the site, the team talks to Francisco again and learns that the mine has been operating illegally in the forest for nearly two decades. No one has been able to shut the operation down, largely because no one knew that it even existed, a fact that underlines just how crucial patrolling the rain forest areas actually is.

As the team continues their conversations with Francisco, they find out something interesting. The miner highlights the fact that the mine isn't really very profitable and probably isn't commercially workable. Park warden Christoph Jaster considers this to be a hopeful sign. He explains: "They just obtain seventy, eighty, or at maximum a hundred grams of gold per month. That's too poor. They are looking for other places to [mine]. That will be a positive moment for us to convince them to leave this place." The question is: will the miners be willing to give up their illegal claims on the land?

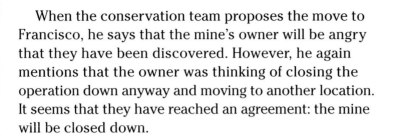

When the conservation team proposes the move to Francisco, he says that the mine's owner will be angry that they have been discovered. However, he again mentions that the owner was thinking of closing the operation down anyway and moving to another location. It seems that they have reached an agreement: the mine will be closed down.

In time, the forest will repair the damage caused by the mine, including the eroded soil and river full of silt; however the mercury pollution will likely have much longer and more dangerous effects. When mercury enters the water system of an environment, it is often transferred to fish and other animals, which is a danger to them. In addition, when these poisoned fish and animals are eaten by humans, people—especially children—can suffer the effects. In the long term, mercury poisoning can cause birth abnormalities, brain injury, difficulties with arm and leg movement and other bodily functions, and sometimes even death.

The team has found—and hopefully successfully shut down—one illegal mining operation, but their mission is not over yet. The rain forest holds even more hidden surprises for the adventurous team. Jaster leads the others to a remote airstrip built years ago by a mining company. Upon their arrival, the team finds two unexpected residents; a couple who are presently living in the forest near the strip. **José**[16] and his wife Madeleina have lived here in the wilderness for 18 years, mining gold with a small **dredge**,[17] and surviving by farming, hunting, and fishing in the rain forest. Although surprised, the two are quite friendly and show the team around their little home.

After surveying the area, the team posts a signboard to make it clear to the couple that this land is a national park now. Unfortunately, nonemployees are prohibited from living in it, so it's not clear what will happen to the couple who have spent 18 years making a home here. The wardens don't want to leave them homeless, but there's no way around the rules, or is there ...?

---

[16] **José:** (ʒuzɛ)
[17] **dredge:** a machine used to dig up sand and mud from a river

Jaster has an idea that may benefit both the couple and Tumucumaque National Park. If things are planned correctly, the husband and wife may not have to move at all. In fact, they too might be able to benefit from the developing park.

Jaster thinks he may be able to offer the pair a salary from the park's government subsidy. The park could then pay them to monitor and maintain the airstrip, the implication being that they would keep it useable for the park's staff and keep illegal users away. The couple seems to be happy with the suggestion and the solution may work well.

The type of idea that Maretti and his team implement in this case is yet another way to get the local residents to support the new reserve. It's important for the administration of the park to work towards involving the local people rather than discriminating against them or ignoring their needs. Such solutions are typical of the way that the ARPA program tries to find positive solutions to difficult problems.

Fact or Opinion?

Look at the following statements. Write 'F' for those that are factual, or 'O' for those that are an opinion.

1. Jaster has an idea that may help Jose and Madeleina. _____

2. Jaster is able to offer the pair a salary. _____

3. The couple is happy about the idea. _____

4. The ARPA tries to find positive solutions to difficult problems. _____

Now, finally, the team from the ARPA program has finished its work and the expedition can return back down the Amazon. There have been a number of important accomplishments during the challenging expedition. The gold miners have been sent on their way and the Wayapi people have agreed to help patrol the new park's borders. In addition to these two achievements, the park's western border has been marked. There is still a lot more work to be done, but the general structure for the park's operations has been started and the basic parameters for monitoring it established. After a lot of hard work and determined effort, it seems that the wardens may well be on their way to maintaining a safe and successful national park.

There are no guarantees that the damage done to the violated areas of Tumucumaque National Park can be reversed, but there are at least signs for cautious **optimism**.[18] This is largely because of the work of the ARPA program. Little by little, the extraordinarily beautiful, lawless wilderness of the Tumucumaque rain forest with its waterways, wildlife, and green forest, is becoming a well-defined and protected national park. The rain forest and the amazing animal and plant diversity in this region now stand a better chance of surviving. Luckily, they have this chance due to the conservation organizations and indigenous peoples who are working hard to save the Amazon together.

---

[18] **optimism:** hopefulness; confidence in a positive outcome

After You Read

1. What is the main purpose of the discussion on page 4?
   A. to provide background information about the Amazon
   B. to introduce what's unique about the country of Brazil
   C. to offer details about numerous species of plants and birds
   D. to explain what scientists do not know about the Amazon

2. On page 6, the word 'critical' is closest in meaning to:
   A. floral
   B. rational
   C. possibly disastrous
   D. abstract

3. Experts in all of the following areas belong to the Amazon Region Protected Areas program EXCEPT:
   A. national parks
   B. wildlife
   C. mining
   D. indigenous peoples

4. What opinion is expressed by Jawapuku Wayapi in paragraph 2 on page 14?
   A. He thinks there are some benefits to mining.
   B. He thinks tribes should cooperate with the government's efforts.
   C. He does not think that the authorities are being straightforward.
   D. He thinks miners will oblige the program's requests.

5. On page 18, the dangerous currents are given as an example of:
   A. why the only people who come here are fortune seekers
   B. how hard the team must paddle to get to their destination
   C. why the team decides to cease their expedition
   D. why others don't often come deep into the rain forest

6. The team constructs a pulley system to get the boat _____ the hill next to the waterfall.
   A. over
   B. in
   C. through
   D. down

7. Which question CANNOT be answered by the information provided on page 25?
   A. What kind of mining is typical in the Amazon?
   B. What forces the water out the other end of the hose?
   C. What happens to the dirt in a sluice box?
   D. What are the environmental impacts of hydraulic mining?

8. To whom or what does 'their' in 'their objectives' refer on page 26?
   A. indigenous peoples
   B. the Amazon Region Protected Areas program
   C. everyone
   D. the Wayapi tribe

9. The writer implies that patrolling for gold mines:
   A. is a necessity
   B. will unify everyone
   C. is silly
   D. is a minimal threat

10. Which of the following effects from mining causes long-lasting damage to the environment?
   A. dirty pools of water
   B. erosion of the soil
   C. silt in the river
   D. mercury pollution

11. Park warden Christoph Jaster recommends that José and Madeleina:
   A. leave their home of 18 years
   B. move to a nearby village
   C. work for the new national park
   D. close down the airport

12. Which achievement did the team NOT make during their journey?
   A. They mediated issues between a miner and his boss.
   B. They marked a western border for the park.
   C. The Wayapi people agreed to work with them.
   D. They shut down an illegal mine.

RAIN FOREST
Medicines

The development of a wide range of new medicines has contributed greatly to a dramatic increase in life expectancy in developed countries over the past 100 years. One quarter of these medicines are derived from plant sources and there is still tremendous potential for the discovery of more useful plant-based drugs. However, at a time when scientists estimate that only 5 percent of the world's plants have been identified, it appears that 25 percent of those plants will become extinct by the year 2050. Therefore, researchers are looking closely at the many possibilities that rain forest plants present as potential sources of new drugs.

LEARNING FROM INDIGENOUS PEOPLES

Along with the loss of valuable rain forest plant species, the rain forest inhabitants who discovered and utilized them are also rapidly disappearing. Since 1900, more than 90 indigenous tribes living in the Amazon's rain forests have been displaced due to agricultural and manufacturing development. With them, centuries of experience working with drugs made from rain forest plants has also disappeared. Only recently have scientists begun to realize how much time and effort can be saved by basing their research on what traditional cultures have already discovered about plants.

CURARE

In recent years, one plant found in South American rain forests has received a lot of attention: curare. Native peoples first used a substance made from this plant to poison their enemies during battle. This powerful drug can cause the lungs to stop working, which results in immediate death. However, tribal people also knew that very tiny amounts could be used to

Total Species Extinctions since 1800

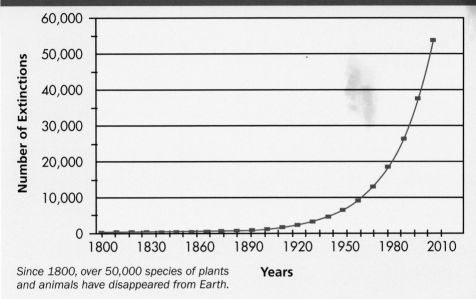

Since 1800, over 50,000 species of plants and animals have disappeared from Earth.

lower a fever or relax the body in order to treat a broken bone. Modern medicine has made good use of this drug. For years it has been employed during medical procedures to relax patients and make surgery easier.

ROSY PERIWINKLE

Rosy periwinkle was originally found only in the rain forests of Madagascar, a small island off the coast of Africa; however traditional societies in different parts of the world found many uses for it. In India it was applied to insect bites; in South America it eased the pain of sore throats; in Hawaii people used it to stop bleeding. Today, it is used worldwide to treat cancer, a disease that causes abnormal changes in the blood or tissue of the body. Cancer drugs based on this plant now account for millions of dollars in commercial sales each year.

CD 3, Track 06

Word Count: 399
Time: _____

Vocabulary List

airstrip (17, 37, 38)
collaboration (26)
crisis (2, 6)
current (17, 18)
deforestation (2, 6)
diplomatic (14)
dredge (37)
erode (2, 3, 25, 34)
exotic (3, 4, 14)
GPS (22)
hose (25)
hydraulic (2, 3, 25)
indigenous (3, 13, 14, 15, 25, 26, 42)
mercury (2, 25, 34)
obstacle (18)
optimism (42)
paddle (18)
paradise (3, 4)
patrol (10, 26, 30, 41)
pulley (21)
silt (2, 3, 25, 34)
sluice (25)
tribe (3, 14, 26)
tropical (4)
warden (2, 3, 13, 33, 37, 41)
wholesale (6)

Metric Conversion Chart

Area
1 hectare = 2.471 acres

Length
1 centimeter = .394 inches
1 meter = 1.094 yards
1 kilometer = .621 miles

Temperature
0° Celsius = 32° Fahrenheit

Volume
1 liter = 1.057 quarts

Weight
1 gram = .035 ounces
1 kilogram = 2.2 pounds